love bites

food for thought and other
appetizing sentiments

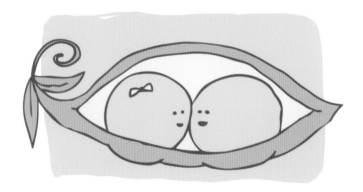

ben joel price

Skyhorse Publishing

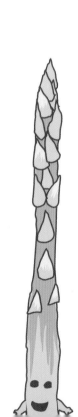

for all the lovers,
the foodies,
and the
foodie lovers ...
enjoy!

'ello cupcake!

who's on top tonight then?

little pluckers

soapea

you can
be so soft
centered –

love chocolate

difference of opinion

you can be such a
little sweet heart! -

- it's 'cos i
love ya!

little gems

carrot top

little hotties

Gaga or Minaj? -

Britney or
Christina? -

- i have no idea what
you just said...

- ahhh, i see

pop tarts!

- sigh!

check out the
birthday suit! -

the exhibitionist

spa tisane

hot and steamy

- gulp!

ménage a trios

-hey, Giusy, let's leave
town and tie the knot

- that's a wonderful
proposal, Walter, but
i simply cantaloupe!

melons

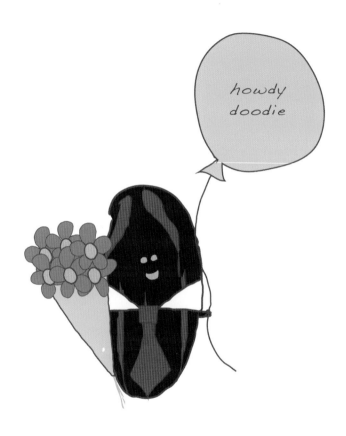

first date

you make
me weak at
the knees,
hotcakes -

love stack, baby!

surprise! –

streaker

sunshine of my life

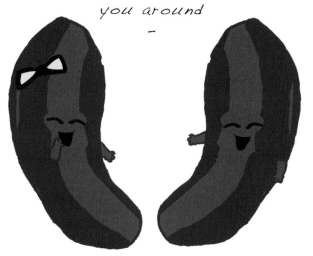

hahahahaha,
there's never a dill
moment with
you around
-

ickle pickle giggle

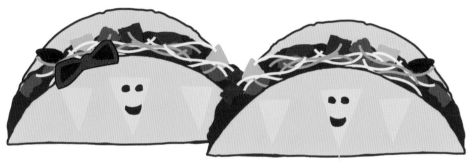

- i'm hot,
  i'm tasty,
i know how to salsa,
 i'm filled with love,
  i'm telling you, i'll
    spice up your
     life forever!

- look, stud,
  let's get one
thing straight, ok?
  i'm nacho girl!

the hard shell

cocktail sausages

– what?

bad hair day

up beet

nacho man

- swoon

dough eyed

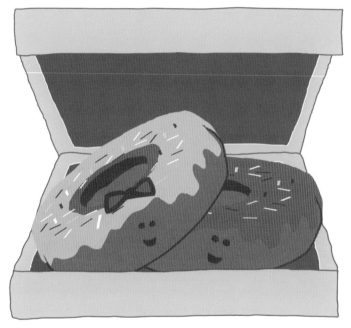

lovers glaze

fast food antics

salad dressing

looking a bit fatty around
the edges, my lovely.
let's get you down to
the gym, trim up a bit -

- right you are,
my love. anything
to stop you giving
me beef about it

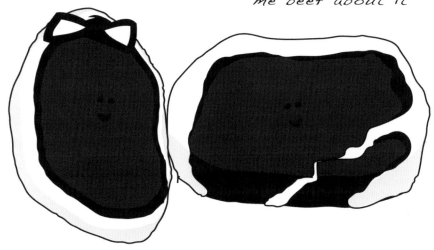

- ah, you can be
a little tender
soul when you
want to be

food fight

awww, come on love,
don't clam up –

shellfish lover

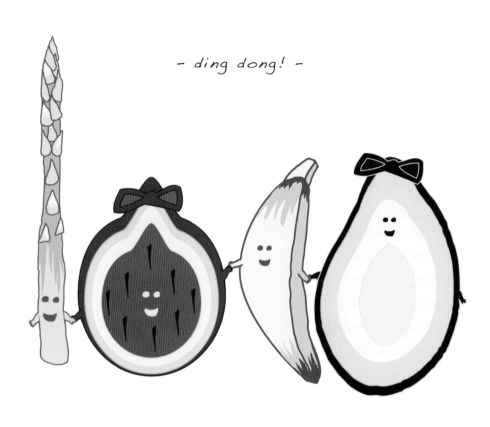

- ding dong! -

swingers

- out and proud! -

plums!

- she has that deep red complexion, but has "perfect skin" apparently. in my opinion, she's vinegar dressed as wine

- jealous much?

- i'm just saying... and i heard she's seedless, too!

sour grapes

um, honey, i don't want to
alarm you, but...
i think it's stuck! -

- oh, quit your drizzling

a sticky situation

this film is
so corny –

– while i
usually value
your film
critique, my
sweet, right
now a little
hush time is
required as i
intend to spend
the rest of
my date with
Ryan Gosling
uninterrupted!

pop off

- udon love me anymore!

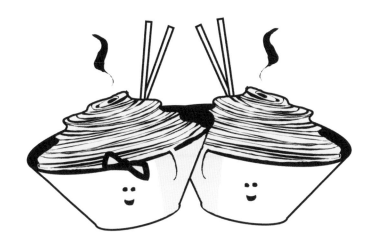

- oh, soba up, hun,
you know i love you oodles!

charmin' ramen

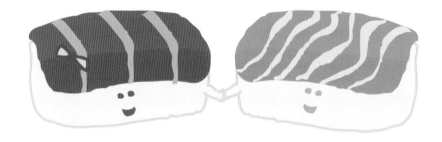

– hello, boys!

pin up

- hey, it's not the
size that counts...

self-assured

you're so mushy -

- give us a smooch

sweet pea

mac and roni,
"couple of the year, 2014,"
celebrating the best years spent
in comfort and sauce

so cheesy

- best legs in town!   - lickin` good, chick!

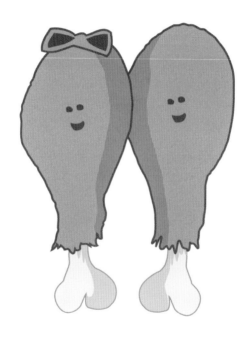

poulet vous?

– sob!

blue cheese

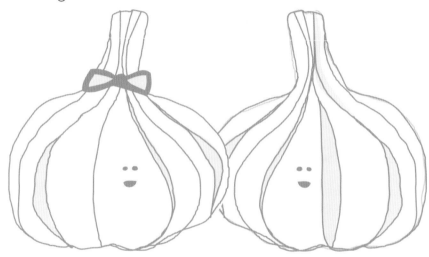

morning breath

premature mastication

- you were
grinding in your
sleep again, pet

run of the mill

apple of my eye

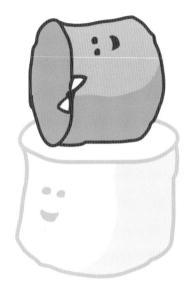

— you're always on my mind, sweetie

big softee

coneheads

deep pan humor

—he's all right,
i s'pose

nice pear

i'm gonna stick with you forever, sugar -

- sounds a little hard to swallow

gum love

you little pea-uty!~

bride and legume

Acknowledgments

Yummy, yummy, yummy, I've got love in my tummy, and I feel like thanking you . . .
Nattles—my brilliant pea with whom I share my pod (told you . . . bit of asparagus!);
my parents—for providing the template for passion and pabulum;
Jan, Nan, Julita, Mr. Hobby, Isabel, and Julie for the sustenance and support;
and finally to food, which I simply couldn't live without.

Still hungry? Continue to spread the love and share a thought with a love bites greeting card
available from: www.symetria.co.uk.

Skyhorse Publishing books may be purchased in bulk at special discounts for sales promotion, corporate gifts, fund-raising, or educational purposes. Special editions can also be created to specifications. For details, contact the Special Sales Department, Skyhorse Publishing, 307 West 36th Street, 11th Floor, New York, NY 10018 or info@skyhorsepublishing.com.

Skyhorse® and Skyhorse Publishing® are registered trademarks of Skyhorse Publishing, Inc.®, a Delaware corporation.

Visit our website at www.skyhorsepublishing.com.

10 9 8 7 6 5 4 3 2 1

Library of Congress Cataloging-in-Publication Data is available on file.

ISBN: 978-1-62636-404-2

Printed in China